YOU AND ME

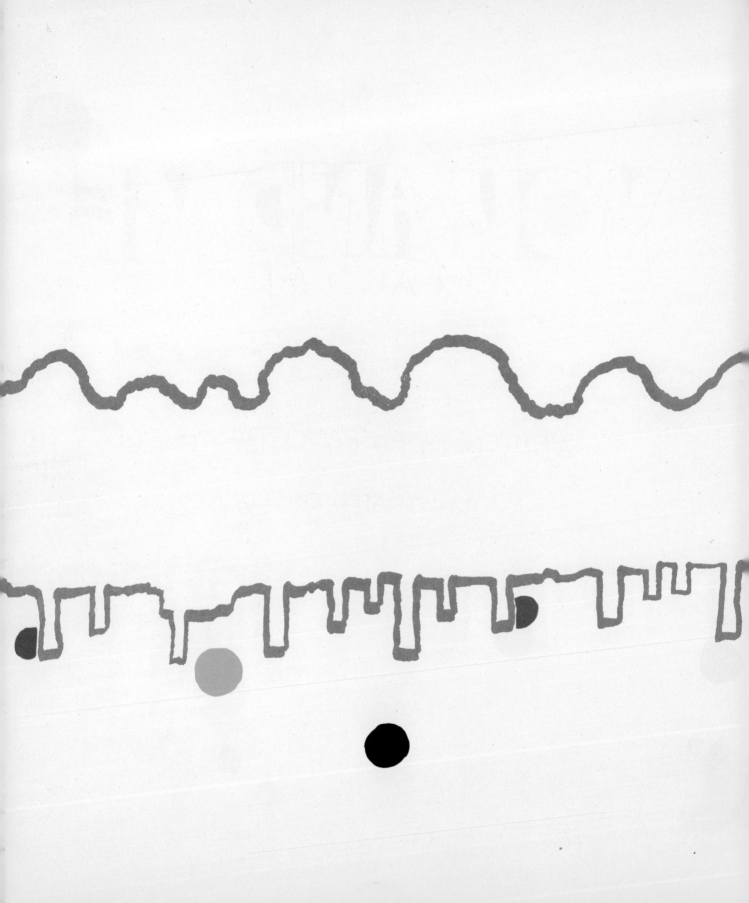

YOU AND ME

WRITTEN BY FLORENCE PARRY HEIDE

ILLUSTRATED BY TED SMITH

CONCORDIA®
Publishing House
St. Louis

Concordia Publishing House, St. Louis, Missouri
Copyright © 1975 Concordia Publishing House

All rights reserved, including the right to reproduce
this book or portions thereof in any form.

Manufactured in the United States of America

Library of Congress Cataloging in Publication Data

Heide, Florence Parry.
      You and me.

      SUMMARY: Explores the concept of each person's
being a separate individual whose thoughts make him different
from anyone else.
      1. Children—Conduct of life. 2. Individuality—Juvenile
literature. [1. Individuality] I. Smith, Ted, ill. II. Title.
BJ1631.H4   233   75-4539
ISBN: 0-570-03436-1   Hardbound
ISBN: 0-570-07791-5   Paperback

HERE I AM

NOW DON'T
FORGET!
EVERY TIME
YOU SEE THE
RED DOT
IN THIS BOOK-
THAT'S ME!

OR

BACK

AND

FORTH

OR AROUND

IF I WANT TO GO FROM HERE ✖

TO HERE ✖ I CAN

LIKE THIS

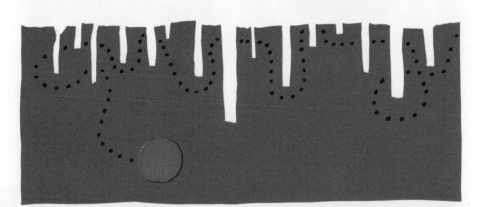

OR THIS

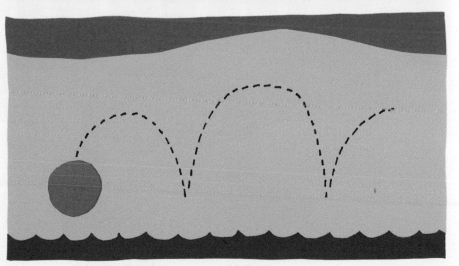

OR
I
CAN
HOP

EVEN
IF
I
DON'T
GO
ANYWHERE

I
CAN
THINK

ABOUT
GOING
SOMEWHERE

I
CAN THINK
ABOUT
SOMETHING
I'D LIKE
TO DO

I
CAN THINK
ABOUT
SOMEONE
I'D LIKE
TO SEE

I CAN HAVE MY VERY OWN THOUGHTS

I
CAN
THINK
OF
LITTLE
THINGS

OR I CAN THINK
OF
BIG THINGS

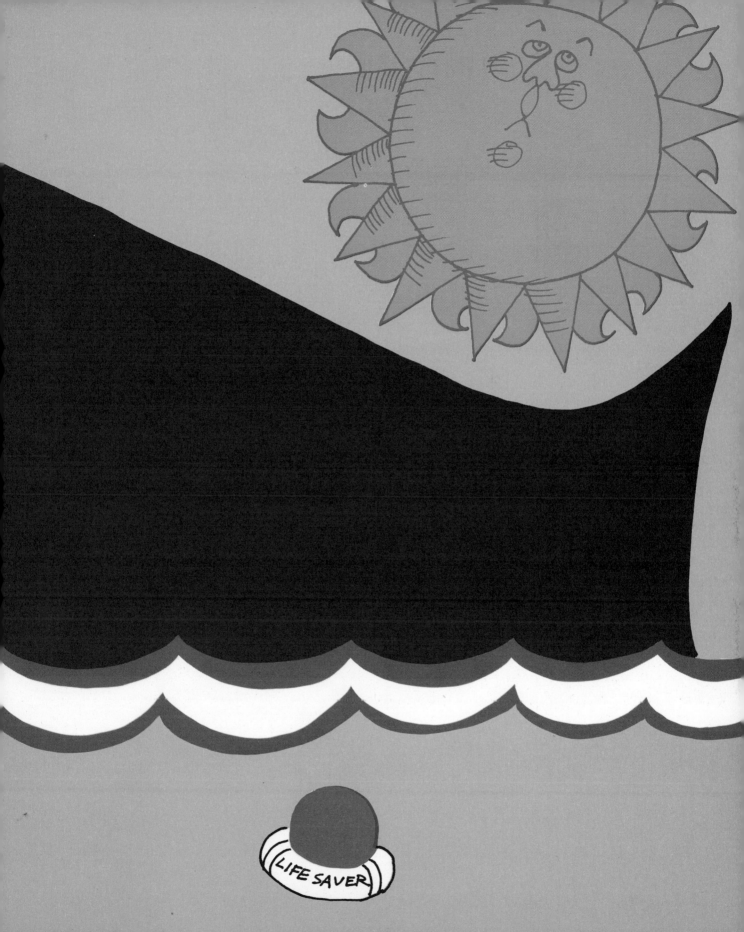

LIFE SAVER

EVEN WHEN I AM SAD

I CAN THINK
OF
SOMETHING
THAT
WILL MAKE ME
FEEL
BETTER

SOMETIMES

I LIKE TO BE ALL BY MYSELF

SOMETIMES

I LIKE TO BE WITH PEOPLE

EVEN IN A CROWD
    I CAN STILL THINK
      WHATEVER I LIKE

SO CAN EVERYONE ELSE

(SOME PEOPLE HAVE MORE INTERESTING
  THINGS TO THINK ABOUT THAN OTHER
  PEOPLE DO)

I LIKE TO BE WITH YOU

WE CAN TELL EACH OTHER WHAT WE ARE THINKING

THAT GIVES US BOTH OTHER THINGS TO THINK ABOUT

EVEN WHEN I CAN'T BE WITH YOU
    I CAN THINK ABOUT YOU
I CAN THINK ABOUT YOU
    AND THE THINGS YOU TOLD ME

1

IT'S WHAT I THINK
THAT MAKES ME <u>ME</u>
THAT MAKES ME
DIFFERENT FROM
ANYONE ELSE

2

IT'S WHAT I THINK
NOT
WHAT I LOOK. LIKE

3

OR
HOW
BIG
I
AM

4

OR WHAT I WEAR.

5

OR WHERE I LIVE

6

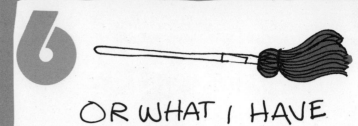

OR WHAT I HAVE

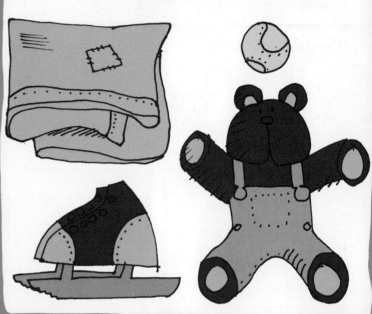

7

IT'S WHAT I THINK
THAT MAKES ME
WHAT I AM INSIDE

IT'S WHAT I AM INSIDE
THAT MAKES ME
<u>ME</u>

8

IT'S WHAT YOU ARE INSIDE
THAT MAKES YOU
<u>YOU</u>

THERE IS ONLY ONE OF ME

THERE IS ONLY ONE OF YOU

GOD MADE ME
        AND HE MADE YOU

WE'RE ALIKE   BUT

GOD MADE EVERY SINGLE PERSON

THEIR OWN PERSON

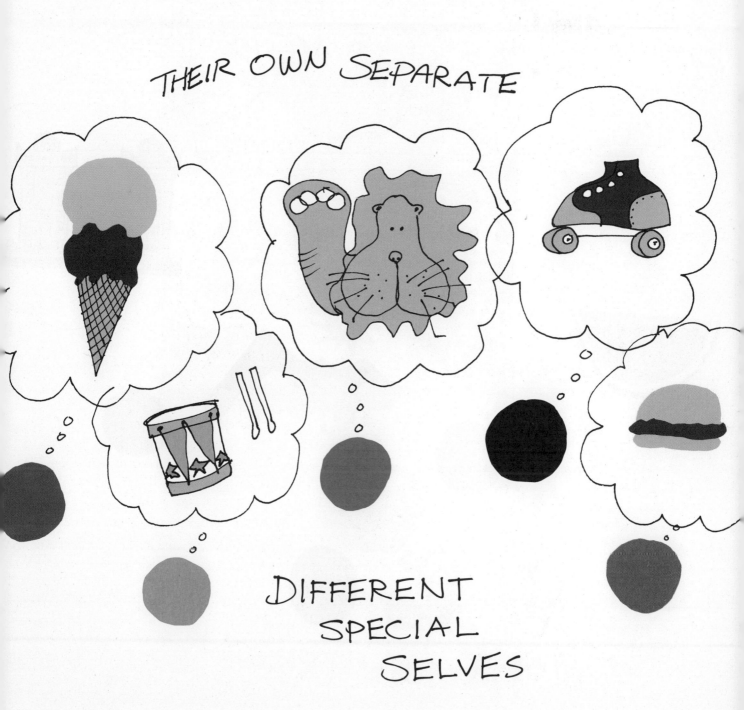

ISN'T THAT WONDERFUL !